Spirit to Heal
Journal of Prayer

By

Dr. Veruschka R. Biddle
&
Dr. Michael H. Torosian

Spirit Press International

SPIRIT TO HEAL – JOURNAL OF PRAYER

Published by Spirit Press International
Copyright © 2003 by M. Torosian/V. Biddle

Grateful acknowledgement is made for permission to reprint material from the following texts:

*12,000 Inspirational Quotations: A Treasury of
Spiritual Insights and Practical Wisdom* (ed F.
Mead). Baker Book House Co., Grand Rapids
© 1965.

*The Treasury of Religious and Spiritual
Quotations: Words to Live By* (eds R Davis & S
Mesner). Stonesong Press, New York © 1994.

The Doctor and the Soul by V. Frankl. Random
House, Inc., New York ©1980.

SPIRIT PRESS INTERNATIONAL
POST OFFICE BOX 544
WAYNE, PA 19087

ISBN 0-9729419-1-6
Cover Design: Butterfly Photo (Courtesy of Sr. Rose)
Printed in the United States of America

Synopsis

This Prayer Journal can provide you with encouragement and hope as you progress through life and travel along your spiritual journey. Prayer places you in direct communion with God. This Prayer Journal can help you understand your journey of healing and access the healing power of God's love - offering hope and inspiration for healing of your spirit. God's Spirit touches ours when we come to Him with our prayers, thoughts, hopes and dreams.

About the Authors

Drs. Michael Torosian & Veruschka Biddle are the authors of *"Spirit to Heal - A Journey to Spiritual Healing with Cancer."* This unique team composed of a surgical oncologist and psychotherapist are touching the lives of many and bringing God's love and healing to this hurting world. Drs. Torosian and Biddle have been internationally recognized for their outstanding work.

3

Preface

When we wrote our first book *"Spirit to Heal - A Journey to Spiritual Healing with Cancer"*, the response was overwhelming from people of all walks of life and from far-reaching corners of the world. The hope, inspiration and healing of one's spirit can impact everyone's life during the most difficult challenges imaginable. One question which consistently arises is how to overcome old patterns of thinking and behavior and to open one's heart to receive and express love and healing. We believe that transformation is possible no matter how deeply ingrained old patterns are in our nature. Constant communication with God and releasing one's fears, pain, and burdens to Him through the power of prayer is essential for spiritual healing.

We hope that this Journal of Prayer will be a daily companion on your life's journey. This prayer journal is written from our heart and hope that it will touch yours. As you go through each day, reflect on God's love and strength and draw upon His power with your every breath and heartbeat. Allow the Spirit of God to illuminate your soul and spirit and know that you are never alone on your journey through life.

When we live in daily surrender, we invite God to participate in every aspect of our lives. We live in a world that is in desperate need of healing, and we believe that healing can only occur by returning to the love of God, our Creator, to Whom all hearts are open and to Whom we will return one day. It is our hope that all will find consolation and comfort in these prayers, especially in the midst of difficult storms in our lives. These storms are an essential part of our journey, and we can trust that God will sustain us through each one.

The greatest challenge is not wishing the storm to be over but in finding the strength to live through the tempest while it is raging. Through this process we learn, grow and transform spiritually and become even stronger. Our prayers are incredibly important for our spiritual healing and the healing of this world.

With this book we invite you on a prayer journey that is deep, powerful and reflective. Remember that the ultimate and deepest healing takes place in your spirit and your spirit is nurtured by the love and grace of God, through prayer.

CONTENTS

Dedication

We dedicate this *"Journal of Prayer"* to all those who provide love, hope, and faith to others in need.   From triumphant celebrations to the most difficult challenges of life, they continue to encourage others to learn, persevere, and heal on their life's journey. May they be blessed and divinely inspired as they proceed on their own path of life and spiritual growth.

Prayer to the Spirit of God

Spirit of God, I pray that You enlighten my soul, bring peace and love to my heart, guide my path and strengthen my will, touch and heal my body, mind and spirit with Your love. Make me an instrument of Your love and peace. Shine through me so I can be a light in this troubled world. Walk with me every step of this journey. Amen

Try to spend just a few moments every day with your eyes closed, calming your thoughts, imagination, feelings and emotions. Calm all your senses to the noises of the world in order to enter into yourself. Go to a quiet place with God and in the solitude of your heart speak to the Spirit of God, saying: "Here I am Lord."

*Many times we find our faith
in times of darkness and with a
broken heart.*

Open your Heart

Relationships depend on the ability of our hearts to reach out and connect with one another. In true friendship, heart speaks to heart and one is free to be oneself. This form of deep union is a gift that God gives us when we open our hearts in love. There is no fear in this kind of love because you can express yourself with honesty and simplicity; you have an openness that is not afraid of hurt, rejection or judgment. You are not misunderstood because you connect on a spiritual level that does not always need words to resonate.

11

Love, kindness, compassion and gentleness are heartfelt emotions and can fully be felt and expressed when we open our heart to God and others. The tragedy of the human condition is that many people have frozen hearts and therefore withdraw rather than embrace their brothers; our actions become less and less loving toward one another. We may feel less vulnerable when our heart is closed, but we cannot truly feel love. Only God's fire of love can melt our heart; for God is love.

Meditation Imagery

Close your eyes and relax your senses and body. Bring to mind a picture of your broken, hurting, or frozen heart. Ask God to touch your heart with His love and feel illuminated in His light. Visualize your heart as it heals, opens or melts.

Feel God's love and the warmth of His healing light deep in your heart. Imagine God's light shining through every part and cell of your body and mind. Rest in this moment and feel revived.

Healing Prayer

I know Lord that I have to open my heart fully to You and others. I realize that I have built a wall around my heart so I will not get hurt but I am also aware that I have shut other people out and that is my way to withdraw or detach. Perhaps my heart is frozen because of pains I have experienced in my life. I invite You into my heart Lord and I ask that You help me to be compassionate, kind, loving and sensitive to the people around me. I ask You to hold my heart in Your hand and protect me from any hurt while I am opening my heart to love. Amen.

Never does the human soul appear so strong and noble as when it foregoes revenge, and dares to forgive an injury.

Edwin Hubbell Chapin

Forgiveness

We cannot heal without Forgiveness. We need to ask God to search our heart for any hidden, repressed or forgotten feelings of resentment, anger, hostility or bitterness. We know that we have truly forgiven if we can wish those who have hurt us well, and we can truly ask God to bless them and release any negative feelings we have toward them. Forgiveness brings peace to our lives and we need a peaceful mind, heart and spirit in order to truly heal. Resentment is not just a feeling; resentment, anger and hostility are actions against our brother and against God. Resentment influences our thoughts, responses and reactions.

The cost of holding onto these feelings can be more anger, doubt, confusion, fear, and broken relationships. All these feelings place unnecessary stress on the body, mind, and spirit and block our spiritual healing.

Prayer Meditation

Begin by relaxing and calming your body and mind, place yourself now in God's divine light and let it shine on you. Sense the warmth of His light and allow the presence of God's Spirit to refresh, revitalize, and calm your mind, body and spirit. Just let it happen, allow God to touch your spirit. Now bring before God all people you wish to forgive and ask God to help you to forgive. All it takes is your willingness to release your negative feelings and God can do the rest. Take a moment and reflect on the forgiveness you need from God. Surrender your heart to God.

Healing Prayer

Lord, I realize that I have been holding on to unresolved feelings of resentment, bitterness, anger and perhaps even hostility. I need You to help me release these feelings that have caused me to respond in ways that are against Your loving nature and mine. I release the people, situations, and my feelings to You and I forgive those who have hurt me and place them into Your hands. Please forgive me for the hurt I have caused others and let Your grace cleanse my heart from all resentment and bitterness. Amen

Prayer is opening our heart and mind to the Spirit of God so He can touch our soul with His love.

All I have seen teaches me to trust the Creator for all I have not seen.

Ralph Waldo Emerson

Developing Trust

*I*t takes trust to have faith and to believe, but many times we have experienced our trust being broken. When we are faced with the pieces of shattered trust, we feel betrayed and may want to withdraw instead of rebuilding what was shattered. We often respond with doubt, fear, confusion, suspicion and look for hidden motives. These responses influence the way we live our lives and can damage our relationships with others. Building trust not only takes time but also the willingness to take risk. One must trust to love, to surrender and to have faith. Without trust we cannot commit ourselves or sustain truly meaningful relationships. Trust is restored by love, acceptance and affirmation that we have a significant place in the heart of God. Trust in God will help us recover when we feel down.

Sometimes we think that God has withdrawn from us, it feels like we are alone, stranded, and abandoned without hope. God is our greatest resource and never abandons us. Sometimes God takes us to a lonely, quiet place for a little while, but only to teach us to "walk by faith and simply trust."

Prayer Reflection

Reflect for a moment on how your inability to trust has affected your faith, your relationships with God and others, and your life. Trust means believing in something you cannot see or feel, trust is knowing that deep inside you is a force, the love of God. That force will always be with you.

Healing Prayer

Lord, I realize that I sometimes find it difficult to trust and therefore I am not able to surrender myself and my life as freely as I should. Whatever broke that trust in me, Lord, I want You to find it and heal it. I want to keep my heart and mind open to the people I love. I am afraid to be vulnerable and I need You to teach me how I can protect myself through You. I realize that most of all I need to learn to trust You so You can touch my life.

It appears that when life is broken by tragedy God shines through the breach.

George A. Buttrick

Brokenness

We wonder sometimes how we could possibly endure when our life and heart are shattered. Just surrender yourself to God and let His wisdom create an even more spectacular masterpiece from the broken parts of your life. You will be stronger and shine more brightly with His light.

We have all experienced the pain of brokenness, a cross to be carried during our life's journey. But there always comes a blessing with our brokenness, we learn who we are and we become aware of our spiritual essence.

Modern medicine has not yet accepted the concept of brokenness, or a broken heart - and yet medical practitioners know it is real. We can feel so fragmented and our life can be shattered and yet people heal from brokenness through God's love. We become stronger, deeper, and more compassionate. Healing brokenness begins by entering into the pain, not fleeing from it. The pain is our spiritual stimulus or motive to recognize the need for healing. Brokenness is more than grief or sadness, it is when we are torn apart by our pain and, precisely at this moment, we have a great opportunity to invite God into our healing process.

A great mystery of our spiritual journey is that our brokenness provides the way directly to the heart of God. He is the One who can make our shattered pieces whole again.

Prayer Reflection

*I*nvite God to walk back with you through your life and in a quiet moment, remember all the times in your life when you felt broken or your life seemed shattered. Let the pain, grief, and sadness surface. As soon as you sense these feelings, let them go from your heart. Release all you feel to God, even your tears are most precious to Him. Now visualize God's divine light illuminating your life and see how it shines. Let the love of God restore you and the light of God heal you. Take a few moments to calm your senses and find peace in your quiet breathing.

What is to give light must endure burning.

Viktor Frankl

Healing Prayer

Lord as I look back I can see and feel the pain of a lifetime, please walk with me and heal my memory, my emotions, my feelings, and my life. Shine Your wonderful, bright and divine light into every piece of my broken self and illuminate my being with Your healing love. Heal the pain of a lifetime in my body, mind, and spirit.

For He will order His angels to protect you and guard you wherever you go. They will hold you with their hands to keep you from striking your foot against a stone.

Psalm 91

Overcome fear as it is one of our greatest obstacles to hope, faith, trust, and spiritual growth.

Overcoming Fear, Doubt and Uncertainty

Remember that you are held safe in God's hand, there is no safer place for you to be. God will provide you with His peace and He sends you people to help along the way. The choice is yours; to trust God that He will be with you always. Surrender your fears and anxious perceptions. With prayer in your life, your fears and feelings of uncertainty become more distant. When we live a spiritual life, we progress from fear to faith, from despair to hope, and from anxiety to serenity.

Prayer Reflection

Enter into a quiet place within yourself and choose trust over fear. Don't let your anxious thought take over, just let them go. Keep choosing peace, trust and faith. Your fears have robbed you of peace and tranquility. Don't allow your anxious mind to control you; you control your mind and thoughts. It will take some time before you have the strength to fight these intrusive thoughts of fear, anxiety and uncertainty. This is part of your spiritual battle and something you must fight. Never surrender to fear, anxiety, despair or hopelessness. Remember, there is no safer place than in the arms of God, where you are held safe. You are loved and protected. We believe that God sends you a special guide, your guardian angel who is assigned only to you. Take a moment and visualize being embraced by his wings and go there whenever you need the strength to fight fear, anxiety or despair.

Healing Prayer

Lord, I thank You for Your protection and for the guardian angel you placed into my life. I thank You for Your loving care. Please protect me from my own weakness, enlighten my mind and my heart so that I will understand that I have nothing to fear. Amen.

The Spirit of God
is
a Spirit of Hope

Hope proves man deathless. It is the struggle of the soul, breaking loose from what is perishable, and attesting her eternity.

Henry Melville

Hope

If we expect nothing from our future, we lose hope. Hope is the most essential element of spiritual healing. Without hope we enter into despair. Hope is interwoven in everything we do. Our prayer needs to express hope for if it does not, we will fail. We need to wear hope like a life jacket that saves us from drowning in fear and despair in times of storms. At these times, God is always close to you; but He does not necessarily tell you what He is going to do. He reveals to you only that He is there. Our greatest challenge is to trust in God, not so much to end the storm but to find in Him the strength to endure the raging tempest. That is hope, a hope that comes from faith and trust that, even in midst of a crisis, we will endure it together with Him.

Prayer Reflection

*W*hy do I find it so difficult to hold onto hope when storms rage all around me? I must realize that God cannot do anything for me until I use my abilities to do what is humanly possible, allowing Him to do the impossible. It takes hope to do that.

Just reflect for a moment and remember all the difficult times in your life when you thought the storm would never pass. You got through, you survived and you learned because these times taught you what you needed to learn. Hold onto God and your faith like an anchor in the storm. Never let go of hope.

Healing Prayer

Lord, I invite You into my doubts, fears, and hopelessness, and I surrender all the thoughts that hinder me from placing my hope in You. Amen.

You must learn to relinquish all your judgments, expectations and convictions until you arrive at the place where there is nothing between yourself and God.

When men surrender themselves to the Spirit of God, they will learn more concerning God and Christ and the Atonement and Immorality in a week, than they would learn in a lifetime, apart from the Spirit.

John Brown

Surrender

Our healing and peace of mind begin when we surrender to God. We cannot surrender to God anything that we don't truly want to release. Surrender means total separation, placing all and everything into His hands. If we truly believe that God is the force that holds everything together, the omnipotent One, surrender would be easy. But to trust God enough to determine our destiny takes faith. Surrendering everything we are, all we have, takes trust in God. Surrender does not make us helpless or dependent, it makes us strong, determined and free.

Prayer Reflection

Why is it so difficult to let go of my fears, concerns, and anxieties, what do I have to lose? How often have I surrendered something to God to find that I had taken it back before He was able to help me? Surrender is not a sacrifice, it is a gift of God's love and His grace.

Healing Prayer

Loving God, I surrender to You with all my heart and soul. I want to open all the deepest places in my heart to You and say "Come in." I surrender all to You, my health, my resources, my work, my relationships, my very being. I surrender my expectations, my motives, my understanding how things should be, my choices and decisions. I surrender my emotions, fears, insecurities, and responses.

Just give me Your love and Your grace, for this is not easy for me. Help me to let go and allow You to take over what I cannot control. Amen.

For nowhere can a mind find a retreat more full of peace or more free from care than his own soul.

Marcus Aurelius

If you have not clung to a broken piece of your old ship in the dark night of the soul, your faith may not have the sustaining power to carry you through to the end of the journey.

Rufus M. Jones

Spiritual Peace

God's peace is felt as tranquility deep within our soul and nothing in our physical world can weaken or damage this feeling. God's peace is a gift to us which we can acquire by simply asking. It is the kind of peace that keeps us calm and safe during the most challenging storms of life. Peace begins in our own heart - if we want peace, we must start creating it ourselves.

Healing Reflection

Cleanse the thoughts of your mind and heart and invite the peace of God's Spirit to dwell in you. Take a deep breath and inhale God's peace, exhale all that has burdened your heart and mind. Slow and deepen your breathing and take in God's peace with every breath. Surround yourself in His divine healing presence and rest in His love for a few peaceful moments.

Healing Prayer

Lord, make me an instrument of Your peace, Your peace is all I need to calm my senses, my body, and my mind. Let Your peace give me rest and a deep tranquility so that I am not overburdened with the events of my life. Your peace gives me strength, thank You, Lord. Amen.

Relinquishing Anger

Anger is an intense emotional reaction, sometimes directly expressed and sometimes repressed. Anger is often hurt expressed and, as such, is more commonly a symptom than a cause of life problems. Anger is a necessary emotion for mature and healthy relationships, when expressed appropriately, but it can also be very destructive. Anger turned inward can cause depression, and outward can turn into rage. Where is the middle ground?

The teachings of Christ are the most profound advice when it comes to resolving anger. He teaches that it is fine to feel angry at times; but that we should not allow our anger to become destructive. He tells us, do not let the sun go down on your anger; in other words, make peace before you end your day. Do not take your anger into the night and carry it into the next day.

Self-control is the key to dealing with anger properly· and to developing our capacity to accept God's love, so that we can respond to others with compassion, grace and sensitivity.

Healing Reflection

Examine your life journey for a moment and reflect on those times when you felt angry. Maybe your anger was justified at the time because someone hurt you, or perhaps your anger made you respond aggressively and unjustly toward others. Have you ever felt angry toward God? Most of us have experienced anger toward God after a loss, crisis or illness. What we need to understand is that God is gracious and loving enough to handle our anger and we need to release our feelings of frustration and anger to Him. Are you willing to let these feelings go?

Healing Prayer

Lord, I admit that I have held onto my anger and that I have expressed my anger in unhealthy and unjust ways to the people close to me. I release all these feelings to You and I ask You to heal my hurts that are at the root of this anger. Please, Lord, forgive me for my anger toward You, especially if my expectations were not fulfilled as I had hoped. Amen

Replace all your pain with love

Gratitude
is the sign of noble souls.

Aesop

Gratitude

*H*ow much in life do we take for granted and how little do we thank Him for all the wonderful blessings in our lives. To feel grateful, our heart must appreciate goodness when it comes, kindness when it touches us, and love when it transforms our lives. Even in our most difficult times, we can see the hand of God at work when we look back. We realize that there was something we learned, or that we were strengthened or transformed through the experience. It hurts when someone close takes us or the things we do for granted. But instead of becoming resentful and angry, express gratitude and understand that no good or loving deed, no matter how big or small, ever escapes the eyes of God, Who will remember, appreciate and bless you.

God gave us a powerful spirit that has the ability to endure and survive incredible trials and to reach out to others in love. Our spirit is unique and forgiving and is an incredible gift from God.

Prayer Reflection

Lord, I have felt so many times that You have taken much from me without realizing all the things You have provided to me. At those times I have lost my way and focus only on myself. I am sorry for what I have taken for granted and I thank You, Lord, for all the Blessings You have given me.

Allow me to see the blessing in everything You place before me and let me be a blessing in the life of someone else today.

Healing Prayer

Lord, please give me the gift of a grateful heart, I know that there are many people who suffer much more than I do. Help me to shift the focus from myself and to see the suffering and pain in the world around me. Unite my suffering with theirs that we all may be together with You on this journey. Thank You most of all for Your love for me, for giving me strength when I feel weak, for the gift of Your grace, mercy and forgiveness, for allowing me through my suffering to be a light in the life of others. Amen.

It is a human prerogative to become guilty and it is a human responsibility to overcome guilt.

Viktor Frankl

Conquering Guilt

Guilt is an emotion that triggers our defense mechanism. There are two forms of guilt: false guilt that incorrectly arises without real cause and true guilt when we feel responsible for a hurtful occurrence. False guilt is not of God and is a painful emotion, based on attitudes of self-punishment, self-rejection, and low self-esteem. Feelings of guilt can weigh heavy on us and can block us from feeling God's presence. True guilt results when we feel responsible for something that has happened. Guilt also demonstrates that we have a conscience, realizing that we may have contributed to someone's pain. Our guilt can bring us close to God in prayer. God invites us to surrender our guilt through the process of forgiveness. When we truly are able to forgive, the feelings of guilt can leave us.

God's plan is not to avoid the pain of guilt but instead to respond in love. Guilt can profoundly affect our spiritual life by making us feel unworthy or unwanted. We must release our guilt to strengthen and restore our spiritual essence.

Healing Reflection

Healing from guilt begins with trust, trusting that God will not only forgive us but also free us from the burden of guilt. God heals us through His grace which is His gift to us. His gift of grace and forgiveness is given in the Spirit of divine love.

Healing Prayer

Lord, I surrender all my feelings of guilt and self-condemnation to You. I choose the love and forgiveness You have for me. Thank You for Your love and understanding and for allowing me to unburden my spirit this way. Amen

God has never promised to reveal to us the path He has mapped out for us, but to trust God means we must take the first step without being able to see where the path will lead us.

Love never gives up,
never loses faith,
is always hopeful, and
endures through every
circumstance.

1 Corinthians 13:7

Love

*W*hen we become aware that God loves us beyond all our human understanding, we are free to go into the world to love others the same way. There is nothing as powerful as the bond of love – true connectedness – understanding one another on all levels, emotionally, spiritually, physically, and mentally. When love is truly giving, it will be returned. Sometimes, however, we are afraid to love or to be loved. But we must realize the greatest of all human needs is not food, shelter, health or possessions – the greatest longing is for love. Love gives us inner strength, hope and purpose.

Remember that love will cast out all fear. Love is the powerful energy that awakens us, re-vitalizes all our senses. Love can heal us, love accepts and gives freely without restriction.

Prayer Meditation

We must be determined to choose "Love" with our whole mind, soul, spirit, and body. Transformation is brought about by love – God's love. When we open ourselves to the power of God's love, we allow Him to melt away any coldness, bitterness and fear. We have to repeat this process until there is nothing left between us and the power of love. Our fear is what closes our heart to love. Surrender your fear to God and give up your expectation to be loved in ways that might be beyond human capacity. Love has no expectations; we receive what we give by grace.

Healing Prayer

Lord,. You have given us a divine commandment to live by – to love as You love, free and unconditional, spontaneous, and accepting.

I ask for the Spirit of God to transform me deep from within. Allow my love to be expressed in extraordinary ways, let Your love flow through me so that my love can touch the hearts of others.

The sole purpose of life in time is to gain merit for life eternity.

St. Augustine

Eternity

*M*any of us are afraid of dying, it is something we don't want to ponder. But at the same time, the most hopeful part of our spiritual journey is the concept of eternal life. We will come to the place where we have nothing to fear, realizing that physical death is the ultimate freedom and destiny of our spirit. We return to the One who gave us life. Our spiritual journey is the way to our eternal home.

The people you love in this life will be with you in eternity and they will greet you when you arrive. We are in spiritual communion with our loved ones in heaven; their love for us is deeper and stronger than ever before. It is only through death that our spirit is completely free and fully healed.

Our spirit is eternal. At death, our spirit departs our body and exists in a realm that is without limits and restrictions – unbounded by the usual restraints of our physical world such as time, space, and gravity. Our spirit remains free, unburdened and protected by God's love for all eternity. Our journey on this earth represents a small fraction of our spiritual existence, but it is real, challenging and transforming. When someone close to us dies suddenly, we may not have the opportunity to say goodbye and tell them how important they were in our life. But it is never too late, they can hear us and know the grief in our heart. Once one's spirit leaves its earthly body, it is completely free to love, to understand and to forgive. One day we will all be re-united and realize that we were never really separated. Our loved ones in heaven are fully aware of us and their love and prayers for us never cease.

Healing Prayer

Lord, I understand in my heart that I have eternal life through You but my mind often enters into doubt and fear. Please help my faith so that I can truly believe that our life goes beyond our journey here on earth. Help me not to fear the hour of my death which is only known to You. While I am still here on this earth, help me make a difference, help me contribute something worthwhile to the life of someone who has lost their faith. Let my actions and words encourage someone who is afraid or lost. Let me be an instrument of Your love and promise for eternity. Amen.

Ask and you will be given,
seek and you will find,
knock and
the door will open to you.

Prayer can move mountains and our prayer moves the heart of God.

Just simply ask. . . . .

God is Love and it is His nature to express His love to us and give us His grace. He wants to bless us, to help us and to strengthen us in times of need. Many feel hesitant to ask God for a blessing or to answer a prayer. God loves when His children come to Him. There is a verse in the scripture that simply says: Ask and I will answer, seek and you will find, knock and the door will open, anything you ask the Father in my name will be given to you.

Novena to the sacred Heart of Jesus

Lord, you have said: "Truly I say to you, ask and it will be given to you, seek and you will find, knock and the door will be opened to you". Today I ask, knock and seek for the grace of ... (communicate your intension). Amen.

Say this prayer as often as you wish, you must be persistent. You can also say this prayer on behalf of someone who has a special need or feels alone or needs strength to overcome a difficult time in life.

Healing Reflection

Just reflect a moment on this great offer we have to simply ask God for anything we need. It does not hurt to ask, and remember God's nature is to bless us. So why not ask Him today, why not seek an answer or pray to Him. God will give you what is best for you. Sometimes it may take some time but our prayers are always heard. We cannot fully love while we still have unforgiveness, anger or resentment in our heart. We must resolve those feelings first, as they block the blessings God wants to give us. Our prayers for healing can remove these blocks to our spiritual growth and transformation. That is precisely what spiritual healing is all about.

A short prayer is all it takes to ask God for a blessing or to make a special request. This is one of the most powerful prayers, since it comes directly from the scripture. God's grace illuminates our life and guides our spirit – all we need to do is ask.

*Let each one remember that he
will make progress in all spiritual
things only insofar as he rids
himself of self-love, self-will and
self-interest.*

St. Ignatius Loyola

Closing

God's divine presence is always with us and fills everything that exists (St. Thomas Aquinas). Allow God to take you on a new level of spiritual awakening and understanding, allow Him to touch all the places in your heart, body, mind, and soul that need His healing love. Remember that He is always with you even when you don't feel His presence. Especially when your emotional life is in turmoil you may find it difficult to feel the delicate sensations of your spirit. But God is always present.

Find rest and peace in these prayers and reflections and believe in the healing power of God's love. In God lies our true security and we can trust Him with everything. As we open ourselves more and more to God's Spirit, we find peace in the silence of our heart. Let this place be your secret spiritual garden, where you can enter any time that you need to be with God. There you find strength, peace, joy, and love. Prayer opens our world to the unlimited capacity of spiritual transformation and healing.

REFERENCES

Davis R, Mesner S (eds). 1994. <u>The Treasury of Religious and Spiritual Quotations: Words to Live By.</u> New York. Stonesong Press. Selected quotations reprinted with permission (Pages 22, 40, 41 and 67).

Frankl VE. 1980. <u>The Doctor and the Soul.</u> New York. Random House, Inc. Selected quotations reprinted with permission (Pages 26 and 51)

Mead FS. 1965. <u>12,000 Inspirational Quotations: A Treasury of Spiritual Insights and Practical Wisdom.</u> Grand Rapids. Baker Book House Co. Selected quotations reprinted with permission (Pages 14, 18, 32, 36, 47 and 59).

Wilkinson BH. 1997. <u>The Daily Walk Bible.</u> Wheaton. Tyndale House Publishers, Inc. (Pages 27 and 55).